In loving memory of Hilary Black, a caring
teacher and wonderful aunt.

Anna Tripp

Hilarious Howlers from School

Michael O'Mara Books Limited

First published in Great Britain in 2011 by
Michael O'Mara Books Limited
9 Lion Yard
Tremadoc Road
London SW4 7NQ

A CIP catalogue record for this book is available from the British Library.

Papers used by Michael O'Mara Books Limited are natural, recyclable
products made from wood grown in sustainable forests. The
manufacturing processes conform to the environmental regulations of the
country of origin.

ISBN: 978-1-84317-689-3 in paperback print format
ISBN: 978-1-84317-819-4 in EPub format
ISBN: 978-1-84317-820-0 in Mobipocket format

1 2 3 4 5 6 7 8 9 10

Cover design by Kate Ransby
Designed and typeset by Envy Design Ltd

Printed and bound in Great Britain by CPI Cox & Wyman, Reading, Berks

www.mombooks.com

Contents

Introduction

Bloopers, clangers and howlers afflict all of us throughout our lives but never more so than during our school years. From the first nervous day at school, through to those final exams, the potential for messing up the answers is ever present and those pitfalls are wide enough for many a pupil to fall in.

This book is a collection of school stories and exam blunders from infant class to university level, as well as a few telling faux pas from teachers and parents themselves. Each one is a real event, conversation or exam answer, although the names may have been changed in order to protect the little innocents. Ranging from spelling mistakes that transform the meaning of a sentence to openly defiant sarcasm and genuine confusion, each entry provides a humorous glance into today's classroom – proof that, for some pupils, their school days are more like school daze.

With thanks to the teachers, pupils and former pupils who told me their stories.

Animal Crackers

Young children have been fascinated by the world's vast array of animals for generations. And they are always eager to find out more about them – from the biggest to the smallest, the cuddliest to the most fearsome. But here are some things that you probably didn't know . . .

'A hostage is a big bird with four legs and a long neck.'

Q: What feature do penguins have?
A: They're funny.
Q: How does this help them survive in their environment?
A: They keep their friends amused so they like them.

'The equator is a menagerie lion running around the Earth through Africa.'

A pupil in Romania had a novel ecological
answer to the question, 'What can we do to
fix the problem of litter in the rivers?'
'Teach the fish to eat garbage,' he replied.

A class in Japan was shown a picture of a
turkey and asked what it was. One pupil put
up her hand and said, 'chicken'. When the
teacher told her to think bigger, she came up
with 'Ah! Super chicken'.

'A giraffe needs a long neck because its head
is so far away from its body.'

A primary school class were discussing the terms for male and female animals when one said that a female dog was a bitch. Another pupil got into the swing of things announcing, 'I know the name for a male dog – bastard!'

'Big flies were hoovering all round the room.'

Work experience in the local council offices was not to a sixteen-year-old girl's liking. When she was asked to write about it at school she reported: 'On my work experience I did not turn up, because they made me litter pick. Then a rakoon come in and eat the book I was givin, so the rest of the week I just chilled in bed. The staff also did not like me. I dont no why.'

When the teacher questioned her about the racoon the girl explained, 'Well, the thing is, Miss, I got given this book to write stuff in for me report, and I left it in the office, an' a racoon broke in, and it was all nibbled round the edges so I kicked off.'

Trying to keep a straight face, the teacher asked her if she was sure it was a racoon, as they are not native to Britain. 'Oh no, hang on,' the girl replied. 'I think I mean a badger.'

'Artificial insemination is when the farmer does it to the cow instead of the bull.'

A teacher was shocked when one of her five-year-olds, who was looking at a book of zoo animals, pointed to a picture and said, 'Look at this! It's a frickin' elephant!'

The teacher took a deep breath and then asked, 'What did you call it?'

'It's a frickin' elephant! It says so on the picture!' said the boy.

Under the picture it read: 'African elephant.'

'To keep milk from turning sour:
Keep it in the cow.'

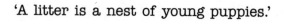

'A litter is a nest of young puppies.'

'He felt all alone almost like an abandoned duck from a family of ducks that had been left behind.'

Q: Why are owl chicks born with feathers?
A: Because otherwise their mothers would mistake them for worms and eat them.

In an essay, one child confidently stated: 'The blue whale is over 31cm long.'

A primary school teacher was about to read
a story entitled *The Speckled
Hen* and asked her class if anyone knew
what 'speckled' meant.
There were a few wrong answers and then
one little boy became very excited and jiggled
around in his seat, convinced he
knew the answer.

  'I know, Miss!' he said. 'It's got glasses!'

Q: Name six animals that live specifically
   in the Arctic.
A: Two seals, four polar bears.

Q: Describe what a quay is.

A: A quay is a baby quail that has leopard spots and is known for its skills in magic and mind reading.

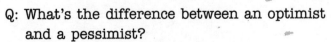

Q: What's the difference between an optimist and a pessimist?

A: An optimist has eight legs.

On an education forum a teacher admitted she had once shouted at a normally sweet twelve-year-old for drawing a penis in his book. After asking him if he was ashamed of himself, the shocked lad looked up and whispered, 'It's a butterfly.'

Weird Science

The science lab is a weird and wonderful place with its test tubes, Bunsen burners and coloured liquids. And it has always held a fascination for children. However, the naked flames and chemicals mean it is fraught with danger and so a close eye needs to be kept on the pupils. It's essential that they know what they are doing. But this list of exam answers from around the world will do little to put parents' minds at ease.

'H_2O is hot water, and CO_2 is cold water.'

'To collect fumes of sulphur, hold a deacon over a flame in a test tube.'

'When you smell an odourless gas, it is probably carbon monoxide.'

Q: Explain one of the processes by which water can be made safe to drink.

A: Flirtation makes water safe to drink because it removes large pollutants like grit, sand, dead sheep and canoeists.

A simpler way of purifying a city's water supply is by 'filtering the water then forcing it through an aviator'.

'Louis Pasteur discovered a cure for rabbis.'

'Charles Darwin was a naturalist who wrote the Organ of the Species.'

'A super-saturated solution is one that holds more than it can hold.'

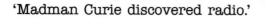

'Madman Curie discovered radio.'

Q: Why do we need iron in our diet?
A: Otherwise we would float away!

If you thought food poisoning was bad, some vegetables can be lethal . . . 'Nuclear leeks are very dangerous.'

Yeah, planes are clever what with all that taking off, flying and landing stuff. But can they clean the carpet? 'Helicopters are cleverer than planes. Not only can they fly through the air they can also hoover.'

'Gravity was discovered by Isaac Walton. It is chiefly noticeable in the autumn, when the apples are falling off the trees.'

There's dead and there's very dead . . .
'A fossil is an extinct animal. The older it is,
the more extinct it is.'

One bright spark had clearly spent a lot of
time reading and watching comic book
adventures. In a science test he came up
with this marvellous 'dynamic duo'. . .
Q: What is an enzyme?
A: A superhero of the cell.
Q: What is a co-enzyme?
A: Enzyme's sidekick.

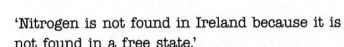

'Nitrogen is not found in Ireland because it is
not found in a free state.'

Worrying signs of an early knowledge bordering on obsession with alcohol came to light with this analysis of water: 'It is composed of two gins, Oxygin and Hydrogin. Oxygin is pure gin. Hydrogin is gin and water.'

The phrase 'drink and be merry' springs to mind after a nine-year-old pupil was asked in her exam: 'Why did the sailors who were suffering from scurvy get a little better when they drank cider?' The correct answer (in case you didn't know) is because cider is made using apples and apples contain Vitamin C. But the pupil's unexpected answer may not have been entirely wrong . . . 'Because they were pissed,' she wrote.

'Momentum is what you give a person when they are going away.'

A seventeen-year-old student had an eye-opening explanation of how turbulence could knock passengers off their feet at a railway station when a train rushes past. 'The eddies suck the passengers off,' he said.

'A magnet is something you find crawling all over a dead cat.'

These were both thought-provoking answers in a junior school exam:

Q: How do you separate a mixture of salt and water?
A: Put the mixture in your mouth and spit out the salt.
Q: What is the process that forms clouds from water vapour?
A: God.

A ten-year-old pupil was confident that he knew the answer to the exam question: 'When is it all right to take drugs?' The proper answer, of course, is: 'When prescribed by a doctor.' But the pupil had the benefit of parental expertise on this one. 'My mum says when you are twenty-six,' he said.

A teacher in Chicago got the giggles when he reprimanded a slovenly boy with this hilarious exchange.
Teacher: 'Pull up your pants! They're defying the laws of physics.'
Student: 'De-what?'

The following cropped up in a physics exam on electricity for fourteen-year-olds.
Q: Give a description of a transformer.
A: It's a robot but is disguised as something else, like a car

During an exam for a course on science fiction, pupils were asked the question: 'A cute girl or guy is making eyes at you at a party. How do you know they are not an android?' One pupil wrote simply: 'If I can't tell the difference, who cares?'

A primary school child showed a commendable sense of logic when asked in a science test what scientists could do to measure or observe how well babies slept. She suggested looking to see whether the baby was snoring. Another answered: 'Mummy says my brother never sleeps and she is losing it.'

'Many women believe that an alcoholic binge will have no ill effects on the unborn fetus, but that is a large misconception.'

Q: Describe one way parents can keep babies
   safe in sunlight.
A: Put a plastic bag over it.

Yeah, it's great,
you don't need to use
nappies either.

During a lesson in biology, a teacher was naming the relevant parts of a skeleton and explained that 'metatarsals' were bones in the foot. An eight-year-old boy turned to a teaching assistant by his side and said, 'Miss, did he say metal arseholes? That can't be right.'

Q: What is a fibula?
A: A little lie

A biology student at a university in the north of England frequently mentioned the 'science of gnomes' in his exam paper. He was actually referring to genomes.

Q: What is a plasmid?
A: A high definition television.

'Three kinds of blood vessels are arteries, vanes and caterpillars.'

'Blood flows down one leg and up the other.'

'The alimentary canal is located in the northern part of Indiana.'

They're not identical twins.

A secondary school biology class was asked, 'What do you get if a horse and a zebra have babies?' and one girl replied 'a leprechaun'. Turned out she meant to say 'unicorn' which still puts her bottom of the class.

Question in a mock biology GSCE exam:
Q: Give an example of movement in plants, and an animal that cannot move?
A: Tryphids and a dead cat.

Nutty Nature

Mother Earth works in mysterious ways to provide the nourishment of life. We may take her for granted sometimes but that's only because we don't fully appreciate just how clever she can be.

'The pistol of a flower is its only protection against insects.'

'To germinate is to become a naturalized German.'

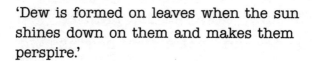

'Dew is formed on leaves when the sun shines down on them and makes them perspire.'

'Mushrooms always grow in damp places and so they look like umbrellas.'

'Rhubarb is a kind of celery gone bloodshot.'

In a Home Economics test on cookery, the
pupils were asked to write down the names
of three typical Scottish dishes.

One pupil wrote, 'A plate, a cup
and a saucer.'

Q: Name the four seasons.
A: Salt, pepper, mustard and vinegar.

Q: How do we get paper from trees?
A: Shake them.

A class of twelve-year-olds were making
cakes but there was a shock in store for the
teacher when they came out of the oven. One
of the boys' cakes was decorated with a
green icing background with a swastika
design made from white chocolate chips.
When the teacher asked him about it, she
was impressed with his knowledgeable reply.

'It's not a nasty sign really, Miss. It was a
Tibetan sign of peace and Hitler stole it!'

That put her straight. Although she did
insist that he explain in to the rest of the
class in case any of them complained to
their parents!

'The Loire valley inspired the chef to cook
delicacies such as salmon, elves and lamprey.'

Medical Marvels

Thank goodness for doctors. We put our lives in their hands and their knowledge of our bodies, medicine, diseases and cures has enabled us to live longer and healthier lives. It's a good job that there are plenty of today's knowledgeable youngsters waiting to step into their shoes. Just take a look at this body of evidence and rest easy about the future health of the population.

'Respiration is composed of two acts,
first inspiration, and then expectoration.'

'The skeleton is what is left after the insides
have been taken out and the outsides have
been taken off. The purpose of the skeleton
is something to hitch meat to.'

Q: Name a major disease associated
   with cigarettes?
A: Premature death.

'When you breathe, you inspire. When you do
not breathe, you expire.'

'The body consists of three parts – the brainium, the borax and the abominable cavity. The brainium contains the brain, the borax contains the heart and lungs, and the abominable cavity contains the bowels, of which there are five – A, E, I, O, and U.'

Q: What is a seizure?
A: A Roman Emperor.

'Germs are sort of small insecks that swim in you when they can get in. Some are called measles but you can't see them.'

'Before giving a blood transfusion, find out if the blood is affirmative or negative.'

Q: Give the meaning of the term
   'Caesarean section'.
A: The Caesarean section is a
   district in Rome.

Worried about the increasing population of the planet? The answer's easy. 'To prevent contraception, wear a condominium.'

Q: What happens to your body as you age?
A: When you get old, so do your bowels and
   you get intercontinental.

Not sure the pupil who wrote the following
explanation should take up medicine: 'For
asphyxiation, apply artificial respiration
until the patient is dead.'

'For drowning, climb on top of the
person and move up and down to make
artificial perspiration.'

Q: What is a terminal illness?
A: When you are sick at the airport.

Don't try this at home: 'To remove dust from
the eye, pull the eye down over the nose.'

Don't worry,
I did first aid
at school.

This seems a bit drastic as well. 'To stop a
nosebleed, put the nose much lower than the
body until the heart stops.'

Manners and decorum are vital above all
else. 'When someone has fainted, rub his
chest or, if a lady, rub her arm above the
hand instead. Or put the head between the
knees of the nearest medical doctor.'

Q: What does 'varicose' mean?
A: Nearby.

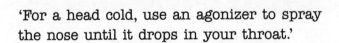

'For a head cold, use an agonizer to spray
the nose until it drops in your throat.'

Q: What are steroids?
A: Things for keeping carpets still on the stairs.

Watch out for those clever people. A professor at a university in the west of England was surprised to be warned by a student that: 'Control of infectious diseases is very important in case an academic breaks out.'

Q: If I stand on my head the blood rushes into it. When I stand on my feet, why doesn't the blood rush into them?
A: Because your feet aren't empty.

'For dog bite: put the dog away for several days. If he has not recovered, then kill it.'

This will make you think. 'The longer you live, the sooner you are going to die.'

It's not all doom and gloom, though. Some people find pleasure in the most unlikely places. 'Heart disease is most popular with the over 55s.'

During a talk about healthy living, the teacher pointed to a picture of a woman's stomach and insides and asked his Year 3 class, 'Can anyone tell me what these are?'

A boy put up his hand and answered, 'They're her intesticles.'

You've all heard about getting blood from a stone. Well, 'The statue of David's arms were taut with sheer perfect muscle – his marble veins bulged with blood.'

'If someone is a vegetable, it is fruitless to try to keep him alive on a machine.'

Q: What's the highest frequency noise a
   human can register?
A: Mariah Carey.

Accusing an opponent of a foul during a game of football, a pupil complained, 'Sir, he kneed me with his elbow.'

Q: Name an individual non-competitive
   activity.
A: Yoda.

On What Planet?

The universe, stars, black holes, the galaxy . . . space is a big subject that has taxed the biggest of brains. But the good news is that it's nowhere near as perplexing as it seems. Just take this crash course and you will soon be amazing your friends with your newfound knowledge.

'The moon is a planet just like the earth, only it is even deader.'

'The earth makes a resolution every twenty-four hours.'

Five-year-old Mal proudly told his mum he had learned all about the planets at school. 'The earth is surrounded by the moon, the sun, Mars and Penis,' he informed her.

'The tides are a fight between the earth and moon. All water tends towards the moon, because there is no water in the moon, and nature abhors a vacuum. I forget where the sun joins in this fight.'

'A planet is a body of earth surrounded by sky.'

Mathematician, astronomer, geographer and astrologer Ptolemy, AD 90–168, compiled lists of planets and constellations. But according to one pupil he left out Uranus and Neptune, ''Cos they had weird names.' Another student took a practical approach as to why Ptolomy didn't record the far planets – ''Cos his computer wasn't good enough.'

During a discussion about sustainable living a thirteen-year-old pupil asked, 'Why don't solar panels work at night, because the moon's like the sun just a little faded?'

Q: Why do we cool down after exercise?
A: To prevent the build up of Galactic Acid.

It Doesn't Add Up

Just when you think you've got it all figured out, the teacher asks a maths question and tells you that you've got the wrong answer. But surely it's as easy as 1,2,3? To sum it all up, there's plus and minuses to this subject. No matter what angle you take or on what scale you measure it, there are two sides to take into account (and three for a triangle). Is that clear?

A fifteen-year-old boy was not to be outsmarted when he got a question wrong. After being told that 18 + 18 was 36, not 32, he replied, 'When did that change?'

'The total is when you add up all the numbers and a remainder is an animal that pulls Santa on his slay.'

An eight-year-old sitting a national maths assessment paper had clearly had enough. When asked, 'Calculate the difference between 294 and 167,' she simply wrote, 'NO!'

A female pupil at a school in Australia was not feeling in great shape when it came to questions of geometry. When the teacher asked how many sides of equal length does an equilateral triangle have? She replied, 'Six.'

Q: You arrive at a bus stop at 2.55 p.m. and the bus comes at 3.20 p.m. How long have you been waiting?
A: Ages.

During an advanced maths class in sixth grade, pupils were learning about the degrees of a circle. But one girl was feeling the heat when she raised her hand and asked the teacher: 'Is it Celsius or Fahrenheit?'

'A line is a length of breath.'

Q: If I gave you ten sweets, then I gave you
   eight more what would you have?
A: Tummy ache.

A twelve-year-old boy tried his best to
placate an angry teacher by showing how
much he had picked up from her lessons.
The teacher was ranting at her class for
being late for her lesson after PE and said,
'How many maths lessons do you have
a week?'
'Three, Miss,' chorused the class.
'And you have been late for two of them,'
said the teacher.
Then one boy piped up, 'Is that three
quarters, Miss?'

'A centimetre is an insect with a
hundred legs.'

The class was responding well to a lesson on metric prefixes, after the teacher explained that 'milli' meant very small and 'kilo' very big. When asked to give some examples of kilo, they answered kilowatt, kilogram and kilometre.

'Good. Excellent,' replied the beaming teacher. Then a hand shot up.

'Yes?' asked the teacher.

'Kilo whale,' said the lad.

A class of six-year-olds were learning about shapes and were told an octagon had eight edges. To help them remember how many edges it had, said teacher, remember an octopus has eight legs. The following day, she drew the shape on the board and asked for the name. One excited boy put up an eager hand and shouted, 'Spidergon!'

During a maths lesson, an eight-year-old boy was dead certain that he knew the answer to the teacher's question.

'What can anyone tell me about symmetry?' asked the teacher.

'It's a place where you bury dead people,' he replied.

'If it is less than 90 degrees it is a cute angle.'

Q: Use the word 'benign' in a sentence.
A: I am eight but I will soon benign.

A group of seven-year-olds were asked to underline a date on their work with a ruler. The teacher began by showing the little darlings what a ruler was and how to use it. One child's effort was decidedly wiggly and the teacher asked why he hadn't followed the instructions.

'But I did miss,' he swore.

'I don't think you did,' replied the teacher. 'Show me your ruler.'

'It's in my pencil case' the lad said.

Teacher looked inside the pencil case but it was empty. 'I can't see it,' she said.

To which he replied, 'It's magic!'

Q: An engineer designed an ocean liner that would extract heat from the ocean's waters at $T_h = 10^\circ$ (283 K) and reject heat to the atmosphere at $T_1 = 20^\circ$ (293 K). He thought he had a good idea, but his boss fired him. Explain.

A: Because he slept with his boss' wife.

A maths teacher was helping an eleven-year-old with simplifying fractions and he got one sum down to $^{13}\!/\!_{20}$.

'Can it get any smaller?' asked Miss.

'No, because you can't divide 13 by anything,' said the boy.

'Good. So what kind of number does that make 13?' she asked, thinking he would know it was a prime number.

Without a pause he replied, 'Unlucky.'

The teacher was puzzled when a young child sitting a maths test drew a detailed picture of a little girl at a desk with her books, ruler and pencil. When the teacher asked why she had done it, she replied, 'It said show your working, Miss.' Trying to keep a straight face, the teacher explained that the note on the paper actually said, 'Show your workings' so that she could see how pupils arrived at their answers.

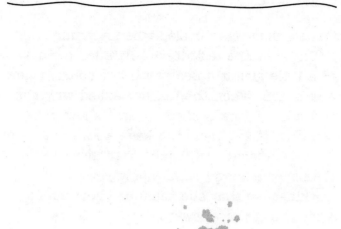

Hysterical History

It may have been a long time ago but that's no excuse for these historic cock-ups. Although some of them are rather more interesting than what really happened.

'Ancient Egypt was inhabited by mummies
and they all wrote in hydraulics. They lived in
the Sarah Dessert and travelled by Camelot.'

A class of eight-year-olds were discussing the
Spanish Armada and its religious causes
when young Marcus put his hand up and
announced, 'The Spanish were Catholics and
the English were prostitutes.'

None of the children laughed but the
teacher did.

'Joan of Arc was burnt to a steak and was
cannonized by Bernard Shaw.'

'Rasputin was a pheasant by birth.'

'Henry VIII rode off on his white whores.'

'Hitler shot himself in the bonker.'

Hard times call for hard remedies: 'In
wartime, children who lived in big cities
had to be evaporated because it was safer
in the country.'

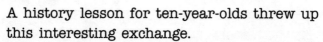

A history lesson for ten-year-olds threw up
this interesting exchange.
Teacher: Can anyone think of a reason for
Elizabeth I to ally with the German Princes?
Child: Well if she didn't, England might have
got bombed by Hitler.

'Sometimes in the war they take prisners
and keep them as ostriges until the war is
over. Some prisners end up in
consterpation camps.'

'Magna Carta provided that no man should be hanged twice for the same offence.'

Q: Where was the American Declaration of Independence signed?
A: At the bottom.

History has a habit of repeating itself. 'In midevil times most people were alliterate.'

'William Tell shot an arrow through an apple while standing on his son's head.'

'Queen Elizabeth was the "Virgin Queen". As a queen she was a success. When she exposed herself before her troops they all shouted "hurrah".'

'The French Revolution was accomplished before it happened and catapulted into Napoleon. Napoleon wanted an heir to inherit his power, but since Josephine was a baroness, she couldn't have any children.'

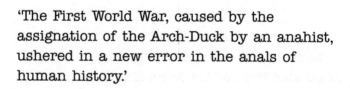

'The First World War, caused by the assignation of the Arch-Duck by an anahist, ushered in a new error in the anals of human history.'

'The sun never set on the British Empire because the British Empire is in the East and the sun sets in the West.'

'Queen Victoria was the longest queen. She sat on a thorn for sixty-three years. She was a moral woman who practiced virtue. Her death was the final event which ended her reign.'

'The Duke of Marlborough was a great general who always fought with determination to win or lose.'

As part of their studies on the First World War, students had to imagine they were soldiers and write letters home from the trenches. 'Dear mum,' wrote one. 'Things are going okay but my hands have been burnt. They are brown and bubbly, just like your cheese on toast.'

'In the Renaissance an unwary rodent became a grand feast.'

This pupil clearly had it licked. 'Sir, isn't Napoleon an ice cream?'

'The nineteenth century was a time of a great many thoughts and inventions. People stopped reproducing by hand and started reproducing by machine.'

'It was an age of great inventions and discoveries. Gutenberg invented removable type and the Bible. Another important invention was the circulation of blood.'

'Sir Walter Raleigh is a historical figure because he invented cigarettes and started a craze for bicycles.'

'Sir Francis Drake circumcized the world with a 100-foot clipper.'

'Christopher Columbus was a great navigator who discovered America while cursing about the Atlantic.'

'The Pilgrims crossed the ocean, and this was called Pilgrim's Progress. The winter of 1620 was a hard one for the settlers. Many people died and many babies were born. Captain John Smith was responsible for all this.'

'One of the causes of the Revolutionary War was the English put tacks in their tea. Finally the colonists won the War and no longer had to pay for taxis.'

'Delegates from the original thirteen states formed the Contented Congress. Thomas Jefferson, a Virgin, and Benjamin Franklin were two singers of the Declaration of Independence.'

'The Constitution of the United States was adopted to secure domestic hostility. Under the constitution the people enjoyed the right to keep bare arms.'

'Abraham Lincoln freed the slaves by signing the Emasculation Proclamation.'

'Abraham Lincoln became America's greatest Precedent. Lincoln's mother died in infancy, and he was born in a log cabin which he built with his own hands.'

A fourth grade pupil in the US told his amused teacher that one of Abraham Lincoln's nicknames was 'Ape Lincoln'.

A head of undergraduate studies in nursing and midwifery in Dundee, was told that 'Vagina Henderson' was one of the first modern nurses of the twentieth century (her name, of course, was Virginia).

'Louis XVI was gelatined to death.'

In the old days, one took pleasure in rather basic conditions. Or, as an eight-year-old wrote in his essay after visiting a reconstruction of an early English settlement, 'They lived in straw huts and there was a lot of rough mating on the floor.'

'Infant mortality was very high, except among the elderly.'

Q: What was introduced in the Children's Charter of 1908?
A: Children.

Q: Outline the importance of the railway in nineteenth-century Britain.
A: The railways were invented to bring the Irish from Dublin to Liverpool where they were promptly arrested for being vagrants.

'The past does not interest me because we know everything about it.'

Holy Moses!

Ah, yes, religion. It's a big subject and much of it is open to interpretation. But most theologians would struggle to follow some of these musings.

'Moses led the Hebrew slaves to the Red Sea, where they made unleavened bread which is bread made without any ingredients.'

A nine-year-old pupil robustly threw herself into prayers: 'Hail Mary full of grace the Lord is with me. Bless me while I go swimming.'

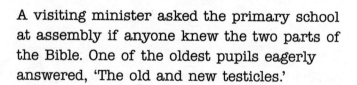

A visiting minister asked the primary school at assembly if anyone knew the two parts of the Bible. One of the oldest pupils eagerly answered, 'The old and new testicles.'

'The Bible is full of interesting caricatures.
In the first book of the Bible, Genesis, Adam
and Eve were created from an apple tree.
One of their children, Cain, asked, "Am I my
brother's son?"'

Teacher: Who brought baby Jesus gifts of
         gold, frankincense and myrrh?
(Silence)
Teacher: I'll give you a clue, there were three
         of them.
Child: The three little pigs.

A teacher had a problem trying to stifle the
giggles after she asked a class of teenagers
about the way Jesus treated non-Jews and
received the reply, 'Jesus was kind to genitals.'

'Solomon had three hundred wives and seven hundred porcupines.'

During a lesson about Easter, one girl of ten was desperate to show off her knowledge and kept putting up her hand to answer questions. When the teacher asked what name was given to the final meal that Jesus shared with his disciples, the little girl again put up her hand. Seeing that no one else appeared to know, the teacher asked the girl to tell the class the answer.

'Sunday lunch,' she replied.

Q: Who was Barrabas?
A: A sunny island in the Caribbean.

Asked to 'outline the importance of the four
Noble Truths to the Buddhist faith', one GCSE
student wrote the following baffling
response: 'Nirvana cannot be described
because there are no words in existence for
doing so. Not non-existence either, it is beyond
the very ideas of existing and not existing.'

Q: What happened to Lot's wife when she left
   Gomorrah?
A: She turned a somersault.

A teacher in Scotland was telling her class a Bible story when she asked if anyone could tell her anything about the Hebrews. Up shot a hand and an eager young boy, answered, 'They're islands near the west of Scotland.'

'Moses went up on Mount Cyanide to get the Ten Commandments. He died before he ever reached Canada.'

Trying to 'relate' to your class in a trendy way can often backfire. When a teacher asked who could name the first book of the Bible, there were blank faces all around. 'Oh come on,' he sighed. 'It's also the name of a rock band.'

Got it, thought one bright spark. 'Guns and Roses.'

Q: Why did the Three Wise Men bring gold to the birth of Jesus?
A: To pay for the hotel.

Q: Why isn't rainwater salty?
A: Because rain comes from Heaven and God's not dirty.

'Solomon was the wisest man of his time, owing to the fact that he had so many wives to advise him.'

One 'scholar' unearthed this rare and hitherto
unknown addition to the Ten Commandments
– 'Thou shall not commit poultry.'

A teacher in a Catholic school was telling her
class how she prays to St Anthony when she
loses things or when she is driving and gets
lost. One of the boys asked. 'Why don't you
just buy a TomTom?'

'Religious people prey every day.'

There was an exotic addition to the stable at Bethlehem when a class was asked to make a crib for Christmas. Halfway through the construction the teacher noticed some papier mâché animals painted with spots.

'What are these?' she asked.

'Leopards,' replied the young sculptor.

'Leopards? At the birth of Jesus?' said the incredulous teacher.

'Yes,' said the boy. 'And they brought sheep with them.'

It was a few moments before she realized that he was mistaking them for 'shepherds'!

Q: What's a catalyst?
A: One of those people that goes to church.

Asked where Jesus came from a five-year-old girl replied, 'Cows.' When the puzzled teacher asked what she meant, the girl replied, 'Well, cheeses come from cows don't they?'

Six-year-old pupil: God created the Earth and all that's in it.
Teacher: Very good. And what happened on the seventh day?
Pupil: God was arrested.

Q: Christians only have one spouse, what is this called?
A: Monotony.

You could try sucking your cheeks in.

Q: Who was sorry when the prodigal son returned?

A: The fatted calf.

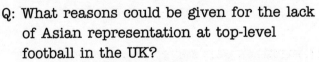

Q: What reasons could be given for the lack of Asian representation at top-level football in the UK?

A: Asians cannot play football on religious grounds, they would have to remove their turbines.

A class of infants in Ireland were asked to draw a picture of the Nativity and the teacher was delighted with their efforts. But she was puzzled by a rather rotund figure that one of her pupils had drawn.

Trying to be diplomatic, she asked the boy who everyone in the picture was.

'Well,' he replied. 'That's Jesus, that's Mary and Joseph and that's Round John.'

Still puzzled, she pressed him for more information. 'You know, Miss,' he said. 'Round John, Virgin Mother and Child.' [sung to the tune of *Silent Night*.]

Wacky World

The world's a wonderful place, isn't it? Full of colour, contrast and breathtaking sights. If you're thinking of going travelling, here's a cut-out-and-keep guide to take with you.

'The climate of the Sahara is such that the inhabitants have to live elsewhere.'

'This summer I went to Egypt and eyed the sphincter.'

'Britain has a temporary climate.'

A student at a university in west London told the senior lecturer in Politics and International Relations that the United States had the most powerful and advanced military in the world, possessing 'highly-developed and powerful marital equipment.'

'The general direction of the Alps is straight up.'

The teacher couldn't believe his ears when a pupil discussing the Middle East mentioned, 'The Best Wank and Gaza.'

'The USSR and the USA became global in power, but Europe remained incontinent.'

Asked to name the great waterfall in Africa,
the class had various incorrect attempts.
'It begins with V,' said the teacher, helpfully.
A hand shot up. 'Miss, Miss, I know.
Viagra Falls.'

Teacher: Can we make an educated
guess why the birth rate is so high in third
world countries?
Child: Is it because there's nothing else
to do?

This exchange in a secondary school left the
geography class unable to work after
dissolving into giggles.
Teacher: Why are there so few petrol
stations in Africa?
Pupil: Because there are hardly any cars.
Teacher: Good. And why are there so few cars?
Pupil: Because there are hardly any
petrol stations.

A university tutor in northern England
received a letter from a former pupil asking
for a reference. It read: 'Will you please be a
referee for a job for which I am appalling?'
The student wanted to be a teacher!

'The UK birth rate is currently increasing,'
a student at a Scottish university wrote.
'We have more than 700,000 new suspects
every year.'

The reception class were enjoying learning about dinosaurs and how they compared to human beings in height. Even better, they got to make some models of them with Lego bricks.

One boy was particularly pleased with his. 'Look, this is my apatosaurus, it's as big as the ten-past-eight building,' he exclaimed.

Puzzled, the teacher asked him where this ten-past-eight building was. 'You know, the big one in America,' he replied.

It was some time before she realized he meant the Empire State Building.

'Miss, the Netherlands, is that where Peter Pan comes from?'

An essay in which a pupil described an utterly desolate and deserted place with no people surprised the teacher with the conclusion, 'it was just like Wales.'

A geography teacher was aware her class of thirteen-year-olds had been learning about rainforests in the previous term and wanted to gauge how much they knew. After getting little response she asked them for one fact about trees. One hand went up and a hesitant pupil offered, 'Birds sit in them.'

Q: In the Hawaiian Islands, there are around 500 different species of fruit fly. Give a reason for this.

A: There are approximately 500 varieties of fruit.

Q: Identify one word from paragraph two which suggests that the mountain does not look welcoming?

A: Scotland.

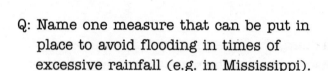

Q: Name one measure that can be put in place to avoid flooding in times of excessive rainfall (e.g. in Mississippi).

A. Flooding in areas such as the Mississippi can be avoided by placing a number of big dames into the river.

Teacher: What does 'summarize' mean?
Pupil: A summarize is a Japanese warrior.

Teacher: And what have you drawn on your
poster about tourism?
Student 1: Guns, Miss.
Teacher: And what has that got to do with
tourism?
Student 2: He thought you said terrorism,
Miss!

A teacher asked the class if anyone knew
what language was spoken in what was then
Yugoslavia.

Leo put his hand up. 'Serbo-Croak,' he
replied.

A Glasgow secondary school teacher was having an interesting discussion on recycling with her pupils, and the subject of the different bins used for the purpose came up.

'What's the advantage of having the different types of recycling in different bins?' she asked.

'It's handy,' replied one tough lad. ''Cos when you're having a fight you know where to get a bottle and when you want to start a fire, you can find the paper.'

The following question cropped up during a college exam on Timber Technology. 'What is Dieldrin, what is it used for and why do environmentalists object to its use?'

One wannabe woodworker answered, 'It is used to kill woodworm and environmentalists object to its use because of the suffering and death it causes the woodworm.'

All Greek and Roman

The ancient civilizations helped form the world with their wisdom, knowledge, artistry and craftsmanship. Let's take a moment to look back at them with this awe-inspiring tribute.

'The Greeks were a highly sculptured people, and without them we wouldn't have history.'

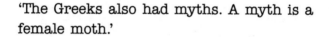

'The Greeks also had myths. A myth is a female moth.'

The Olympic Games used to have some odd events, according to this child. 'The Greeks ran races, jumped, hurled the biscuits and threw the java.'

'Actually, Homer was not written by Homer but by another man of that name.'

Helen of Troy was surprisingly beautiful given that she 'launched a thousand ships with her face'.

'Socrates died from a dose of wedlock.'

Young Connor knew what BC stood for. 'Before computers,' he told his teacher.

'Eventually, the Romans conquered the Greeks. History calls people Romans because they never stayed in one place for very long.'

Teacher: Who can name a Roman God?
Boy: Herpes, Miss.

'Julius Caesar extinguished himself on the battlefields of Gaul.'

Q: Name one of the early Romans' greatest
achievements.
A: Learning to speak Latin.

'Nero was a cruel tyranny who would torture
his subjects by playing the fiddle to them.'

It wasn't all blood and guts by way of
entertainment. It seems the ancient Romans
enjoyed more genteel spectacles. 'The
Romans breathlessly watched the fight of the
gladiolas in the arena.'

'The name of Caesar's wife was Caesaria.
She was above suspicion.'

Q: Describe some of the work a slave would
do in ancient Rome.
A: Anything the boss tells him to do.

'The most famous Greek landmark
is the Apocalypse.'

'When Caesar was dying, he gasped out: 'Tee
hee, Brutus.'

Musical
Mayhem

These kids seem to be singing from
their very own songsheet, turning
sweet music into a cacophony.

'Johann Bach wrote a great many musical compositions and had a large number of children. In between he practiced on an old spinster which he kept up in his attic.'

'Bach died from 1750 to the present. Bach was the most famous composer in the world and so was Handel.'

'Handel was half-German half-Italian and half-English.'

'50 Cent is a rape artist. He goes up and down the country raping.'

An A level music student was describing minimalist music. 'The music is rather repetitive, leading to a general feeling of monogamy.'

Herr Beethoven, the concert starts in two minutes.

'Beethoven wrote music even though he was deaf. He was so deaf he wrote loud music. He took long walks in the forest even when everyone was calling for him.'

A teacher in the US thought it would be fun
to take some of his old vinyl records in to
school to show his young pupils. When he
pulled a record out of its sleeve it was
greeted by the remark, 'Wow! That's the
biggest CD I have ever seen!'

An English teacher in Georgia, US, was
explaining how an actor could change their
performance if things weren't going well, for
instance if someone fluffs a line or misses a
cue. Trying to put this in context, she asked
the sixteen-year-olds if any of them played
in the school orchestra. One girl said she
played the violin and the teacher told her,
'Let's say you're in the middle of a
performance, and your G-string breaks . . . '

School 'Trip'

It's bad enough keeping them housetrained at school but taking them on a trip is just asking for trouble. Let loose like excited chimps, it's no wonder that they get up to monkey business.

The baboons made a big impression with this ten-year-old girl after a visit to the zoo. She later wrote in her essay, 'We went to the monkey and bamboo encloser, and a bamboo came up the glass and kind of shoved its butt on the glass. Its bum was rainbow colour. It was so weird because it had colour bands around the bum hole.'

A parental/guardian consent form for a European trip asked if the child had any special dietary requirements. One came back with the reply: 'Spicy Chicken Pizza.'

A group of female pupils were returning
from a supermarket in Austria carrying
large watermelons.

Their teacher shouted across the car park,
'Girls, where did you get those big melons
from?'

Cue red face from teacher, strange looks
from passers-by and giggles from the girls.

While on a fieldtrip to a farm, one little boy
pointed excitedly to a type of deer that
resembled an antelope. 'Ooh, miss!' he said.
'Are those the cantaloupes?'

On a trip to an aquarium, an excited primary school child shouted across the crowded room, 'Miss, come and look at the testicles on this octopus!'

On a week-long educational science trip, a class in their first year of secondary school was divided into four groups – protons, photons, neutrons and electrons. The physics teacher explained the functions of all of these during the week away and was pleased that they all seemed to understand.

Two years later, when taking the same group away (now in their third year) a pupil asked the teacher, 'Please, Miss, can I be a crouton again?'

A class was being shown around a grand Georgian house as part of their history project. When they entered the dining room, the well-spoken guide informed them that the silver dishes in the centre of the table were for the condiments.

'What,' said one child, 'did they have AIDS in those days too?'

On a visit to a scientific university, during a long and rather complicated talk from a scientist about greenhouse gases and their effects on the environment, the children were beginning to flag. Even the teachers were struggling to understand it all. After a long twenty minutes, the scientist asked if anyone had any questions. Quick as a shot, one child replied: 'No, we're all bored. Let's go.'

A boy of six was wide-eyed in amazement
when he arrived at the sea lion enclosure on
a trip to the zoo. 'Wow! Look at that giant
slug!' he shouted.

The school party had a lovely time in Paris
where they visited Disneyland. On their
return, the Modern Languages teacher asked
one of the girls how they had enjoyed their
trip to France.

The puzzled girl replied, 'We weren't in
France. We were in Paris.'

Mad Metaphors and Silly Similes

Sometimes kids try too hard when it comes to creative writing. They want to be descriptive but just can't find the right words to use. Thankfully, teacher has taught them about metaphors and similes.

A twelve-year-old girl got quite excited when describing the weather in her essay. 'The thunder was like a herd of elephants coming on your face.'

'The little boat gently drifted across the pond exactly the way a bowling ball wouldn't.'

'McBride fell twelve stories, hitting the pavement like a hefty bag filled with vegetable soup.'

'Her hair glistened in the rain like a nose hair after a sneeze.'

'The hailstones leaped from the pavement, just like maggots when you fry them in hot grease.'

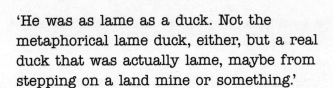

'He was as lame as a duck. Not the metaphorical lame duck, either, but a real duck that was actually lame, maybe from stepping on a land mine or something.'

'The young fighter had a hungry look, the kind you get from not eating for a while.'

'Even in his last years, Granddad had a mind like a steel trap, only one that had been left out so long, it had rusted shut.'

'The plan was simple, like my brother-in-law Phil. But unlike Phil, this plan just might work.'

'The ballerina rose gracefully en pointe and extended one slender leg behind her, like a dog at a fire hydrant.'

A thought-provoking list of proverbs cropped up after six- and seven-year-olds were asked to complete these well known sayings:

* Strike while the . . . insect is close.

* Don't bite the hand that . . . looks dirty.

* Better to be safe than . . . punch a grade 7 boy.

* If you lie down with dogs, you'll . . . stink in the morning.

* You can't teach an old dog new . . . maths.

* The pen is mightier than the . . . pigs.

* An idle mind is . . . the best way to relax.

* Where there's smoke there's . . . pollution.

* A penny saved is . . . not much.

* Two's company, three's . . . the Musketeers.

* Don't put off till tomorrow what . . . you put on to go to bed.

* Laugh and the whole world laughs with you, cry and . . . you have to blow your nose.

* You get out of something only what you . . . see in the picture on the box.

'Pandemonium not only reigned, it poured.'

'He spoke with the wisdom that can only
come from experience, like a guy who went
blind because he looked at a solar eclipse
without one of those boxes with a pinhole in
it and now goes around the country speaking
at high schools about the dangers of looking
at a solar eclipse without one of those boxes
with a pinhole in it.'

'He had a deep, throaty, genuine laugh,
like that sound a dog makes just before it
throws up.'

'I was nervous, but at last I gathered up my
guts and spoke to him.'

This pupil surely underestimated the pain of divorce. He wrote, 'The revelation that his marriage of thirty years had disintegrated because of his wife's infidelity came as a rude shock, like a surcharge at a formerly surcharge-free ATM machine.'

'He was as tall as a six-foot, three-inch tree.'

Shaky-speare

When it comes to one of the world's greatest playwrights, pupils are on shaky ground. With his complex language, unusual characters and unfamiliar concepts, students of the Bard often lose the plot entirely.

A teacher told his Year 10 class that they were going to watch a production of *Macbeth* on video. A boy put up his hand and, with a quizzical expression on his face, asked, 'Sir, you know how you said that Shakespeare wrote the play four hundred years ago? Well, does that mean that the video is going to be in black and white?' Strangely enough, it was.

Talking his class through what would be on their test paper, a teacher remarked, 'When you get to the Shakespeare question –' but he was interrupted by a child exclaiming, 'Shakespeare! We've not done any Shakespeare! We've just been doing that *Much Ado* thing.'

One student was at pains to stress that there was no homosexual aspect to *Much Ado About Nothing*. 'Benedick has a hard choice to make as he loves Claudio, but not in a gay way 'cos that would make the play even more complicated. Also gay people didn't really exist in those days.'

Another student thought the bard was making much ado about nothing when it came to love. 'According to Shakespeare love is hard but I don't agree. When you love someone, stuff the hard times, they don't matter.' She then went on to say, 'Personally I think Benedick made the wrong choice. I would choose my mates any day of the week.'

And then there was this concise response to a question about relationships in the play. 'Loving someone isn't easy and neither is this question.'

This student had clearly had enough of Shakespeare's olde English and flowery language and letteth off steame thus: 'How is this of any use to us! Why learn Shakespeare when no one speaks like that any more. Fair enough learning it for drama – that's acting, but asking us a question about it is pointless. No one in this world speaks like that any more so surely teaching us something which will help – like writing letters and stuff – but Shakespeare is really pointless. I hope the world will realize this one day.'

'Benedick and Beatrice didn't stick to the rules of Courtney Love.'

After trying her best to work things out, this pupil just blamed the writer for not being up to scratch. 'But then again, we have to remember this was written by Shakespeare and Shakespeare doesn't always make much sense, so it's no surprise Benedick is confused by Beatrice's outburst.'

'Claudio and Hero's relationship gets ruined in their first marriage because of an evil trick caused by Don John (the bastard).'

The Tempest also raised tempers. 'Stephano sounds like an evil person and he is a boi. The problem with Shakespeare is I don't understand the words and when you read it it sounds like you don't make sense.'

Teen-speak mixed with Shakespeare when one student said that after hearing of his wife's death Macbeth, 'goes into full-on soliloquy mode.'

A third-year pupil used very 'un-Shakespearian' language when telling how Lady Macbeth – after the murder of Duncan – 'Ses to Macbeth, "sort your head out".'

Homespun philosophy spurred Macduff on to his revenge against Macbeth according to one pupil who reasoned, 'As my mum always sez, "wot goes around comes around."'

Lady Macbeth got an eyeful when, according to one pupil, she asked Macbeth 'to show her his manhood'.

Richard III was a cool dude for the time. He was 'the type of guy who has cruise control on his car, an 80-inch plasma screen TV and a pumping surround-sound system.'

'Richard III was a player.'

But he had his critics. One child marked, 'Conclusion' at the end of her essay and wrote, 'From looking at all of the evidence I would say Richard is a tw*t.'

'Richard was a big weirdy pervert because he wanted to marry his niece. That's dirty and not right.'

'Richard is quite a boring person – all he wants to do is have sex and kill people.'

Hollywood has a lot to answer for. Leonardo DiCaprio got a lot of youngsters interested in Shakespeare after his starring role in Baz Luhrmann's movie, *Romeo + Juliet*. But one fourteen-year-old girl got the film mixed up with another of his hit films and, in her exam paper, wrote that Romeo drowned on the *Titanic*.

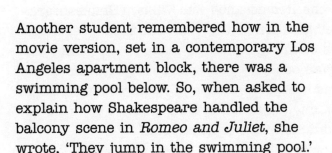

Another student remembered how in the movie version, set in a contemporary Los Angeles apartment block, there was a swimming pool below. So, when asked to explain how Shakespeare handled the balcony scene in *Romeo and Juliet*, she wrote, 'They jump in the swimming pool.'

In a *Romeo and Juliet* essay a fourteen-year-old referred to the huge feud, asserting that 'they were fighting because the Montagues hate the Copulates.'

Perhaps the most honest answer in a SAT exam was, 'I don't f***ing know.'

A GCSE answer stated: 'The greatest writer of the Renaissance was William Shakespeare. He was born in the year 1564, supposedly on his birthday. He never made much money and is famous only because of his plays. He wrote tragedies, comedies, and hysterectomies, all in Islamic pentameter. Romeo and Juliet are an example of a heroic couplet.'

One examiner marking a Shakespeare paper was amused by the following, which took up the majority of an A4 sheet: 'Oi marking person. There are 3961 bricks in the wall in front of me.'

I Blame the Parents

Some parents could do better when it comes to setting a good example to their little darlings. Here are some letters sent to schools by parents explaining their child's absence.

'My daughter has had a bad knight in bed, and has something wrong in her tummy.'

'Please excuse George for being absent yesterday. He had a cold and could not breed well.'

'Chloe has been off for the last three days because she had a twenty-four-hour bug.'

'Please excuse Roland from PE for a few days. He fell out of a tree and misplaced his hip.'

'Please excuse Jimmy from PE today as the rabbit ate his plimsoles.'

'Katie was absent yesterday because she had a stomach.'

'Please excuse Lindsay from taking part in her PE lesson today as she has come down with a very severe case of womanhood.'

'Dear Sir, please excuse Jason for being absent as he was sick and vomited up the High Street.'

'Please excuse John for being absent Jan 28, 29, 30, 31, 32 and 33.'

'Jenny will not be coming to school today because she had jim yesterday and she can hardly walk.'

'Maryann was absent December 11–16, because she had a fever, sore throat, headache and upset stomach. Her sister was also sick, fever and sore throat. Her brother had a low-grade fever and ached all over. I wasn't the best either, sore throat and fever. There must be something going around. Her father even got hot last night.'

That's horrible! Go and clean yourself up.

'Johnny was off sick yesterday because he got diarrhoea through the hole in his balaclava.'

A letter to the head was signed: 'Yours insincerely'.

A mother was becoming increasingly
frustrated and angry as an assistant head
teacher read out a list of examples of her
son's bad behaviour at school. When she
started to become abusive, the teacher said
that he was going to 'terminate' the
interview. The mother raised her eyebrow
and replied, 'Oh, so you are the f***ing
Terminator now, are yer?'

A Scottish teacher was shocked when a little
lad in her class offered the following
explanation for an absence. 'I couldn't come
to school as Celtic won the league, there was
a lock-in at the pub to celebrate and
everybody was too pissed to get up yesterday
to get me ready!'

Plain Speaking

The English language has numerous peculiarities and pitfalls that can lead to many a comical misunderstanding. Sometimes shocking, often endearing, these gaffes are sure to make you smile.

A girl pupil at a tough inner-London school went home crying to her mum after the teacher had criticized her. The following day her furious mum marched up to the school with her daughter in tow and confronted the headmaster.

'What's the problem?' he asked.

When the mother asked the girl to repeat what the teacher had said to her, she said, 'She called me a f***ing, lying doormat!'

The shocked head summoned the teacher to his office and demanded an explanation. 'What exactly did you say?' he asked.

The teacher replied, 'I just told her that her faculties were lying dormant.'

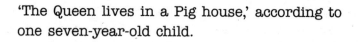

'The Queen lives in a Pig house,' according to one seven-year-old child.

In a recent creative writing exam one pupil wrote, 'Suddenly the teacher backfired in the corridor.'

A student writing about pond life stated, 'There are many orgasms in a pond.'

An A level psychology class had been learning about the nature of dreams. In the following lesson one girl asked, 'Are we learning about those lurid dreams again?' The teacher assumed she meant lucid but, as they had been told that dreams are often about sex, she may have meant exactly what she said.

After a PSHE (Personal, Social and Health Education) lesson, a nine-year-old ran to their mum and shouted, 'Guess what – we did drugs with Miss today.'

A Scottish student completing an English assessment wrote, 'Some drug addicts and alcoholics steal things so that they can sell them to get money to feed their hobbits.'

... and don't come back without some grub.

After a playground argument, a young pupil reported his classmate's misdemeanour to a member of staff. He told her, 'He swore, he said the R word.' It wasn't until some time later the teacher discovered what the R word was – *arse*!

Shortly before moving up to secondary school, a class was asked to write an essay about their childhood. One story concluded, 'I have enjoyed my childhood and I'm now looking forward to adultery.'

A primary school teacher in England was trying to get his class to come up with the word 'fair' during a discussion. He was surprised it hadn't sprung instantly to mind and was beginning to get exasperated. The deputy head popped her head round the door just as he shouted, 'Come on! Think of a four-letter F-word!'

Q: What is the definition of agoraphobia?
A: An intense fear of pubic places.

A primary school teacher made her
staffroom colleagues weep with laughter
when she showed them a charming story
written by one of her little charges. It was
about a wizard who had golden penis
(pennies) in his pocket and kept getting it
out to show to people who all said, 'wow'.

As a school broke up midweek, a primary
teacher was amused when one of his pupils
asked him, 'Have you got the rest of the
week off, or do you have to come in for
incest days?'

An attractive female teacher was leaning over a desk marking some work when a six-year-old pupil piped up, 'Big ticks!'

Mishearing the lad she looked up in shock, checked her top to see if she was revealing too much cleavage, and said, 'Pardon, James?'

'Big ticks,' he said, and pointed to the sheet she was marking. To her relief she saw that her red biro ticks were indeed bigger than usual.

Just then another voice piped up from the back of the class, 'My mum's got big tits and she drives a bus!'

A teacher in Scotland was telling her pupils how to form an adjective from a noun by adding the word '-less', e.g. 'thoughtless'. The children came up with a few examples but when they ran out she prompted them with the question, 'What would you call someone who has no teeth?'

One little lad stuck his hand up and answered confidently, 'Gumsy.'

'In last year's Christmas concert Linzi played the main prat. I played one of the smaller prats and I would like to have a bigger prat this year.'

A young lad writing about what he would pack to take on holiday finished his list with 'and most impotent, pants'.

Not Quite Write

Every English Literature teacher
strives to instil a deeper understanding
of the classics and inspire admiration
for the fine words of authors,
playwrights and poets. Sadly, it
doesn't always work.

'Writing at the same time as Shakespeare was Miguel Cervantes. He wrote *Donkey Hote*.'

A student at a university in the west of England was analysing author Margaret Atwood's novel, *The Handmaid's Tale*, and explained that the story showed 'how patriarchy treats women as escape goats'.

'John Milton wrote *Paradise Lost*. Then his wife died and he wrote *Paradise Regained*.'

A senior lecturer in journalism in a university in the south of England enjoyed a feature by one budding writer about 'complimentary' medicine. And a wannabe fashion writer described the subject's sense of style as very 'sheikh'.

'A fairy tale is something that never happened a long time ago.'

'*Beowulf* is an anonymous medieval poem written in the eighteenth century by Robert Cotton.'

'Letters in sloping type are in hysterics.'

'The greatest writer of the futile ages was Chaucer, who wrote many poems and verses and also wrote literature.'

'A great person never said this, but they should have.'

Q: In *Pride and Prejudice*, at what moment does Elizabeth Bennet realize her true feelings for Mr Darcy?

A: When she sees him coming out of the lake.

A group of ten-year-olds had been studying Charles Dickens and had watched some scenes from *A Christmas Carol*, where Scrooge holds onto the fur trimming of the Ghost of Christmas Past and they fly out of the window. One lad later wrote, 'Santa jumped out of the window while the old man grabbed his furry bits.'

Pip may have been an orphan who had no *Great Expectations* in life but he felt quite comfortable as a man after he 'built a beautiful house and had genital flowers swaying in the breeze.'

An eight-year-old boy describing Peter Pan wrote that he wore 'a green hat and had green tits.' Presumably he meant tights.

'In *Lord of the Flies*, the boys are sorted out by a high Iraqi.'

Q: The dog chased after the ball. What comes
   at the beginning of the sentence?
A: A capital letter.
Q: What comes at the end?
A: His tail.

Q: Use the word 'judicious' in a sentence to
   show you understand its meaning.
A: Hands that judicious are as soft as
   your face.

After reading a story to her class of primary school children, the teacher asked them if anyone could tell her the name of the person who writes books. One little girl put up her hand and said 'author'.

'Well done,' said the teacher 'And does anyone know the name of the person who draws the pictures?'

Up went another hand and a little boy said, 'Author's pal!'

Excuse Me?

If some children lack imagination when it comes to creative writing, it may be because they've used it all up thinking of excuses for late homework. The following are genuine stories spun to teachers in the hope of getting away with it.

A teacher was asking some of her Year 9 students why they hadn't brought in their homework. Tired of silly excuses, she asked them to be honest.

After some standard 'I forgots', a girl at the back said, 'Well, Miss, I was copying Jade's on the bus and left my book on the seat!'

The teacher was speechless but, as she later commented, 'I *had* asked for honesty.'

'It was a cloudy weekend and I have a solar-powered calculator.'

'I couldn't do my homework because I was kidnapped by terrorists.'

'I don't have my homework today because it flew into my fan and got torn up.'

'Homework? I thought you said housework, so I went home, washed up and hoovered the living room.'

One fifteen-year-old, who had had the same weekly timetable for over six months, told his teacher, 'I didn't bring my homework in because I forgot we have maths on Thursday.'

'Sorry I can't return my homework today, but I put it on top of the TV so I wouldn't forget it and the TV blew up.'

This one is not just an excuse – it actually happened to the author of this book!
'I put my history folder on top of the car and my mother drove off, the folder fell into the road, and the pages scattered to the four winds.'

'Suzie was late for school because her alarm clock got eaten by a giant herd of raging elephants.'

'I'm late to class because there are too many stairs.'

A student sent an apology for missing an exam to a college examinations manager in Warwickshire. The email ended with the line: 'I am sorry if this caused you any incontinence.'

Logical
Explanation

Answers from the class may not always be the ones the teacher is looking for, but sometimes you just can't argue with the logic.

Q: What did Mahatma Gandhi and Genghis
   Khan have in common?
A: Unusual names.

A reception teacher told a four-year-old in
her class, 'Johnny, take your pencil out of
your mouth.'

To which he replied, 'It's not in my mouth.
It's in my nose.'

The following appeared as a question in a
physics degree exam at the University of
Copenhagen.
Q: Describe how to determine the height of a
   skyscraper with a barometer.
A: You tie a long piece of string to the neck of
   the barometer, then lower the barometer
   from the roof of the skyscraper to the
   ground. The length of the string plus the
   length of the barometer will equal the
   height of the building.

A keen Newcastle United fan who had just got a new pet couldn't wait to tell his teacher.

'I've got a new rabbit' he said excitedly. 'I wanted to call it Shearer but my mum said that you can't call a rabbit Shearer.'

'So what did you call it then?' she asked.

The child replied, 'Alan.'

A boy of seven asked his form tutor if she could tie his shoelaces.

'What's the magic word?' she asked.

To which he earnestly replied, 'Abracadabra.'

A teacher scolded a lad of fifteen who was sporting a baseball cap in the corridor.

'Wearing hats indoors is against school rules,' he told him. 'Hand it over please.'

To which the student replied, 'No sir, I wasn't *wearing* it, it was just on my head.'

A teacher in Lousiana, US, remembers this exchange with a young pupil in elementary school.

Teacher: Write a letter to the Easter Bunny.

Pupil: There is no Easter Bunny, my mother told me so.

Teacher: Well, pretend. Use your imagination.

Pupil: What's that?

'A graveyard is where dead people live.'

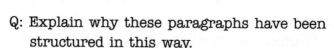

Q: Explain why these paragraphs have been structured in this way.

A: I don't know, I didn't write the booklet.

Teacher: What do you want the new baby
    to be?
Primary school pupil: Human.

After a child asked her if she had an eraser,
a primary school teacher said she didn't and
asked the class instead. One boy put his hand
up and said he had one but when the teacher
asked to borrow it he said, in all innocence, 'I
don't have it here. It's at home. I thought you
just wanted to know who had one.'

Q: Redundancy is often an unpleasant and unexpected event in someone's life. Give two examples of unexpected life events.
A: 1) Death 2) Reincarnation.

Q: Name something important that wasn't around twenty years ago.
A: Me.

A primary school SATs paper had pictures of various shapes such as a square, a triangle and a rectangle. The students were asked to name them.

'Bill, James, Sarah, Mary,' wrote one child.

In his finals at drama college a student had to answer the tricky question, 'What is drama?' He waffled on for a page about the suspense and tension before adding his thoughts on the element of surprise that every drama needs. The last word on the page was 'So . . . '

On the next page, in huge red letter taking up the whole sheet, he wrote, 'THIS IS DRAMA.'

Unfortunately, the dramatic conclusion was that he failed the exam.

One student may just have had a point when he wrote, 'The Prime Minister has the power of disillusion.'

In a language class for eleven-year-olds the teacher asked if anyone knew the French for 'butter'.

'I do miss,' said one eager lad. 'It's Lurpack.'

In answer to the question, 'What is the French word for door?' a seven-year-old replied, 'J'adore.'

Computer Crash

New technology is the domain of the young and schoolchildren know more about bits, bytes and hard drives than most grown-ups will ever know. But even the computer whiz-kids can get it wrong.

A computing class were told to copy a passage into a document. One pupil put his hand up and, pointing to the original text, told his teacher. 'I can't find this funny little thing.'

Teacher asked, 'What funny little thing?'

'It looks like a tiny tadpole,' replied the boy.

Puzzled, the teacher looked at where the lad was pointing and said, 'That's a comma!'

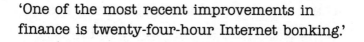

'One of the most recent improvements in finance is twenty-four-hour Internet bonking.'

Q: Explain the term 'free press'.

A: When your mum irons your trousers for you.

An A level exam asked pupils where, apart from the mainframe of a computer, they would store data. One replied, 'In a cupboard.'

Q: What is media?
A: One of those rocks that flies in space.

An eight-year-old child asked miss if she would be using the 'Attractive Whiteboard'.

Patent Attractive Whiteboard

Q: Joanna works in an office. Her computer is a stand-alone system. What is a stand-alone computer?

A: It doesn't come with a chair

Answer given by an ICT GCSE student to a question about the Data Protection Act.

Q: Give one example of an illegal use someone could make of the data.

A: You could use it to track someone down and devour their soul!

Who'd Be a Teacher?

Dealing with classrooms full of unruly kids and trying to impart knowledge at the same time is not the easiest of jobs, and some kids can present a tough challenge. Here's a little tribute to the brave men and women who take on the pupils of the world every day.

A twenty-one-year-old working as a classroom assistant in a primary school asked what the children had done at the weekend. One little girl replied, 'It was my mum's birthday.'

The assistant told her, 'That's a coincidence. It was my mum's birthday too.'

'How old was your mum?' asked the girl.

'Forty,' the assistant said.

Looking puzzled, the child stared for a moment then asked, 'Are you older than your mum?'

A secondary school teacher was intrigued when her colleagues referred frequently to the 'craft students' in their classes. Innocently, she asked which crafts the pupils were studying and was met with a chorus of laughter. 'They're not really studying a craft,' explained one fellow teacher, 'It stands for "Can't Remember A F***ing Thing".'

A music teacher who was taking a guitar lesson saw that one of his pupils had a loose string on his instrument. Just as the headmaster popped his head round the door, the unfortunate chap was heard to say to the girl, 'Let me put on your G string.'

A departing primary school teacher was surprised to receive a card from one of her pupils that read, 'I am sorry you are living.' She is still hoping it was just bad spelling!

In 2008, leading UK exam board, OCR
(Oxford Cambridge and RSA Examinations)
made a schoolboy error when it printed
several answers to its GCSE music paper on
the back of the question papers. The paper
included a copyright section that credited
composers such as Handel next to the
question number, thereby providing the
answer. Another question asked which
instrument a soloist was playing and the
copyright listing included the word 'violin'.

A secondary school teacher was getting
increasingly frustrated by a pair of fourteen-
year-olds who were larking about in her
class, stealing each other's pencils, rulers
and calculators. In the end she blurted,
'Boys, is it really necessary for you to play
with each other's equipment?' Cue fits of
giggles for the rest of the lesson.

Staff members of one school in Sussex were surprised when a supply teacher came into the staff room moaning about the ignorance of the junior class she was teaching. 'You'll never guess what they said in their maths lesson,' she exclaimed. 'I asked them what five times zero was and they all said zero!' Embarrassed coughs all round.

During assembly a teacher praised some inventive children who made some kites during an activity session. She began to explain their 'cunning stunts' but got the beginning of each word mixed up. That's one spoonerism the school never forgot.

The teacher of a class of fifteen-year-old boys was getting cross because every time she turned her back a hum of chat started up. Eventually she said, 'Every time I turn to write something on this board there is no reason for you all to have a mass debate about it.'

Needless to say, she is still trying to live the phrase down.

A maths teacher asked her class of fourteen-year-olds whether they were feeling happy.

They answered that they were, then one of them piped up, 'Are you going to crush our souls with algebra now?'

A teacher in Pennsylvania was reading the book *Mick Harte Was Here* by Barbara Park to her twelve-year-old class. It's the sad story of a girl dealing with the death of her brother and ends with the words, 'It can give you the shivers if you think about it too much.' But the unfortunate teacher rather spoiled the poignant ending when she read, 'It can give you the shitters if you think about it too much.' Sad thoughts soon gave way to hysterical laughter.

The day after he spotted her waiting for a bus, a shy pupil at a Shropshire school came up to his teacher and said, 'I saw you at the bus stop today.'

'That's right,' she replied.

He continued: 'First I thought you were a lady, then I saw you were Miss Barker.'

A mother of a nine-year-old girl was shocked at a parents' evening when a concerned teacher showed her what her daughter had written in her class diary. It read: 'Last night my daddy was looking after us and he put us to bed and read us a story and then he pissed on the cat.'

The mother assured the teacher that she would get to the bottom of it and the following morning she asked her daughter why she had written the remark.

The girl insisted that it was a genuine account of what had happened, explaining: 'But Mummy, it's true. Daddy read us a story and when he was going downstairs he saw that the cat was under the bed and he went "pssst, pssst, pssst" to get him out.'

A teacher in Glasgow was exasperated when one teenage girl in her French class asked, 'Miss, how come I can't understand you when you speak French, but when I'm watching *'Allo 'Allo!* I know exactly what they're saying?

Risky Business

In every school lurk the Alan Sugars and Donald Trumps of the future – children whose innate business sense will inevitably take them far. Then there are the others.

'After several years his business began to flush.'

Q: Define the term 'intensive farming'.
A: It is when a farmer never has a day off.

A college lecturer was coming to the end of a course on various types of business and decided to run a test on her students. The first question asked them to explain what a 'sole trader' was. One answer came back, 'Someone who sells shoes and sandals.'

Q: Explain the word 'wholesaler'.
A: Someone who sells you whole items – e.g.,
a whole cake.

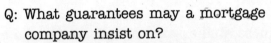

Q: What guarantees may a mortgage
company insist on?
A: If you are buying a house they will insist
that you are well endowed.

Q: In a democratic society, how important are elections?

A: Very important. Sex can only happen when a male gets an election.

In a business studies exam pupils were asked to assess a fashion house's choice to locate its factory near Birmingham.

Q: Is Birmingham the right location for this type of business?

A: No. People from Birmingham aren't very fashionable.

A professor from a university in London was informed by one of his students that part of the reason for the downfall of building society Northern Rock was 'the laxative enforcement policies' of the regulator.

A young lad filling in a sheet for his careers advisor seemed confused about his future. He wrote, 'I would like to be an accountant but you have to know a lot about moths.'

Q: What name is given to an individual who possesses a new enterprise, venture or idea?
A: Captain Kirk.

Q: Suggest an advantage to video conferencing.
A: You can't smell bad breath via video.

'Market fluctuations are continually rising.'

Q: What is a co-operative?
A: It is a shop which is not as expensive as M&S.

Q: Define the term 'microbusiness'.
A: A shop that sells microwaves.

Acknowledgements and Sources

With thanks to many current and former teachers for their stories, as well as friends for their reminiscences.

And with a special thank you to Jim, for lending a hand when I needed it most.

Publications

Times Educational Supplement
Sunday Sun
Newcastle Herald
The Glasgow Herald
The Washington Times
The Independent
Daily Mail
The Guardian
The Times

Books

Hunt, Cecil *Howlers* (1928)
Richmond, Frank M. *School Yarns and Howlers* (1934)

Websites and forums

http://community.tes.co.uk
http://atechdiva.wordpress.com
http://www.turnerink.co.uk
http://www.allscottishteachers.co.uk
http://community.tes.co.uk
http://teachers.net
http://www.timeshighereducation.co.uk

ACKNOWLEDGEMENTS AND SOURCES

http://bombay.indology.info
http://lordsoftheblog.net
http://www.funny-english-errors.com
http://psy.otago.ac.nz
http://paperspast.natlib.govt.nz
http://goodteacher.co.nz
http://jeffreyhill.typepad.com
http://bussorah.wordpress.com
http://www.teacher-1-stop.co.uk
http://www.scribd.com
http://chriswondra.com
http://www.innocentenglish.com
http://www.stuffmystudentssaid.com
http://www.webenglishteacher.com
http://www.ems.psu.edu
http://theteacherstales.com
http://madtbone.tripod.com